Let's Eat

Teacher's Choice Series

Donna Chicca
Bakersfield, California

Illustrations by
Steve Pileggi

Dominie Press, Inc.

The development of the *Teacher's Choice Series* was supported by the Reading Recovery project at California State University, San Bernardino. All authors' royalties from the sale of the *Teacher's Choice Series* will be used to support various Reading Recovery projects.

Publisher: Raymond Yuen
Series Editor: Stanley L. Swartz
Illustrator: Steve Pileggi
Cover Designer: Steve Morris
Page Design: Pamela S. Pettigrew

Published by:

Dominie Press, Inc.

5945 Pacific Center Boulevard
San Diego, California 92121 USA

ISBN 1-56270-537-7
Printed in Singapore by PH Productions.

Our family went for a ride in the car.

We rode and rode and rode.

"Let's eat!" said Mom.

"Let's wait!" said Dad.

We rode and rode and rode.

"Let's eat!" said Brother.

"Let's wait!" said Dad.

We rode and rode and rode.

"Let's eat!" said Sister.

"Let's wait!" said Dad.

We rode and rode and rode.

"We are back home," said Dad. "Let's eat!"

About the Author

Donna Chicca earned an M. Ed. from California State University, Bakersfield in Early Childhood Education. She is in her third year of teaching Reading Recovery™ at Wayside School in Bakersfield, California. She has a wonderful husband and three beautiful children.